HOW TO DRAW HORSES

Lucy Smith

Designed by Fiona Brown
Illustrated by Chris Chapman,
Jamie Medlin and Adam Hook

Cartoon illustrations
by Jo Wright

Contents

About this book

Horses are some of the most beautiful and inspiring animals to draw, but also some of the most difficult because of the complicated nature of their body structure and proportions.

In this book you can find out how to draw lots of different types, from a peaceful, grazing mare and foal to a fiery bucking bronco.

A good way to get an idea of how a horse's lines should flow in a drawing is to trace a picture like the one on page 3. You can then move on to drawing a horse from scratch using the simple method described on pages 4-5.

The pictures in this book use five types of drawing materials: either pencil, watercolor, gouache, felt tip pens, or colored pencils. Examples of the first four are shown on the right, while page 3 gives some tips about using colored pencils.

Pencil works well for detailed drawings, as it is easy to control.* Pencils are coded according to how hard or soft they are.** This head was done mainly in a soft HB, with the dark eye and mane drawn in a softer 2B. ▶

Watercolor paint gives a soft, subtle look which works well for young animals like this foal. The base layer needs to be applied carefully on damp paper.

Gouache paint is fairly thick and gives a picture a solid finish. Unlike watercolor, you can apply the dark colors first, then add paler highlights on top.
▼

◀ Felt tip works well for cartoons, as you can apply areas of flat, very bright color quickly and easily. Thin black felt tip gives a strong, clear outline.

2 *Pencil is also good for quick sketching (see page 8).
**Hard pencils are ones from H up to 9H. Soft ones are anything from HB to 9B.

Tracing and coloring

The lightest color in the coat should be applied first. Use colored pencils, or a thin layer, or wash, of watercolor on damp paper.

Let the base color show through on parts where the light falls. This adds shape and makes the coat shine.

Flowing strokes work best for the mane and tail. Use a gray base, with dark brown on top.

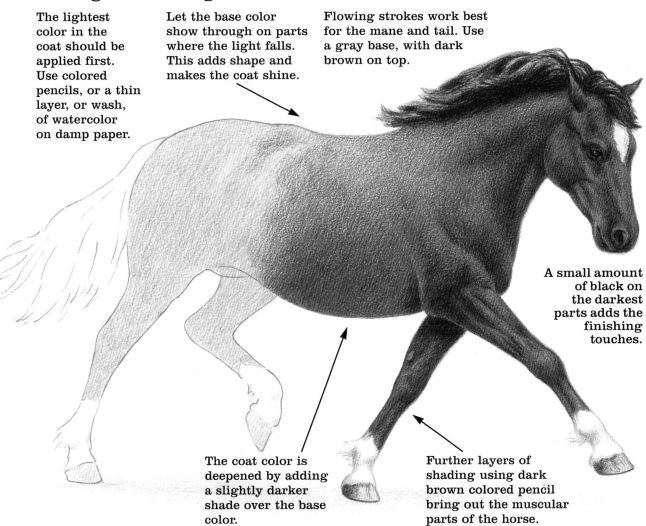

A small amount of black on the darkest parts adds the finishing touches.

The coat color is deepened by adding a slightly darker shade over the base color.

Further layers of shading using dark brown colored pencil bring out the muscular parts of the horse.

Lay a sheet of thin tracing paper over this picture. Fasten it with two strips of masking tape* to hold it still. Trace the image carefully with a fairly hard pencil, such as a 2H.

To transfer the image to thicker paper, turn the tracing paper over and go over the lines in a soft pencil, such as a 2B. Turn the sheet back over and lay it on the thicker paper.

Redo the outlines in harder pencil. The soft pencil on the underside will be transferred to the paper beneath. You can then refine the outlines before applying color as above.

*You can buy masking tape from art shops or grocery stores. It can be taken off paper without tearing it.

Drawing a horse

A horse's shape is complicated, so to make your pictures look right, it is important to get the different parts in proportion. In pencil, try copying the horse below by doing the shapes and lines shown in red first, then the green, then the blue.

All the yellow lines on the sketch are the same length. You can use these lines to check that different parts of the horse are the correct size in relation to each other.

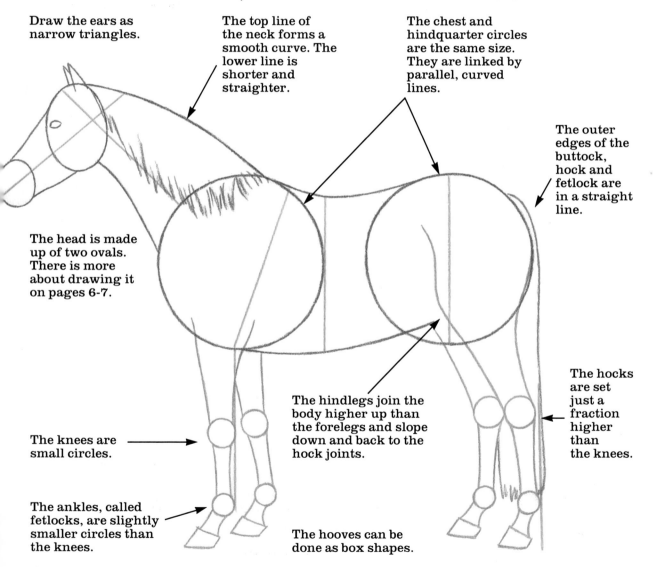

Draw the ears as narrow triangles.

The top line of the neck forms a smooth curve. The lower line is shorter and straighter.

The chest and hindquarter circles are the same size. They are linked by parallel, curved lines.

The outer edges of the buttock, hock and fetlock are in a straight line.

The head is made up of two ovals. There is more about drawing it on pages 6-7.

The knees are small circles.

The hindlegs join the body higher up than the forelegs and slope down and back to the hock joints.

The hocks are set just a fraction higher than the knees.

The ankles, called fetlocks, are slightly smaller circles than the knees.

The hooves can be done as box shapes.

Getting a good finish

Here you can see how to complete the picture to get a realistic effect. Refine the outline, then erase the lines you no longer need before applying a pale yellow-gold as the base color. Gradually deepen the coat color with layers of darker gold and brown. If using paint, as here, let each layer dry before applying the next.

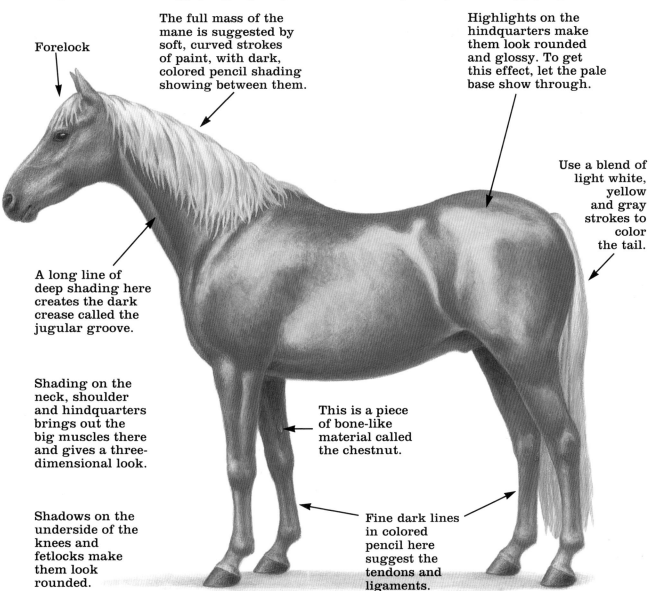

Forelock

The full mass of the mane is suggested by soft, curved strokes of paint, with dark, colored pencil shading showing between them.

Highlights on the hindquarters make them look rounded and glossy. To get this effect, let the pale base show through.

Use a blend of light white, yellow and gray strokes to color the tail.

A long line of deep shading here creates the dark crease called the jugular groove.

Shading on the neck, shoulder and hindquarters brings out the big muscles there and gives a three-dimensional look.

This is a piece of bone-like material called the chestnut.

Shadows on the underside of the knees and fetlocks make them look rounded.

Fine dark lines in colored pencil here suggest the tendons and ligaments.

Horses' heads

The head is the horse's most beautiful and impressive feature, so drawing it in detail can produce lovely pictures as well as being good practice. Here is a way to build up the head in stages. Opposite are four different types to try, with hints on getting the right look for each one.

Stage 1

Do a large oval for the main part.

Add a small overlapping oval for the muzzle.

Stage 2

Construction lines help to position the features.

This distance...

...is nearly the same as this distance.

This is about half the distance above.

Stage 3

Refine the outlines and erase the construction lines.

Apply pale gold as the base. Let the paper show through on the lightest parts.

Stage 4

Shading inside the ears fills out their shapes.

For the mane, do fine gray and fawn strokes with white space between them.

Add very fine, curved eyelashes.

Paint the eyes black and add a tiny white dot, or highlight, to give them luster.

Dark shadows inside the nostrils give them depth.

Soft brushstrokes give a velvety feel to the muzzle.

Add the veins as dark lines.

Palomino horses are golden with white or flaxen manes and tails.

A pony

The eyes are placed halfway down the main oval and at the sides of the head.

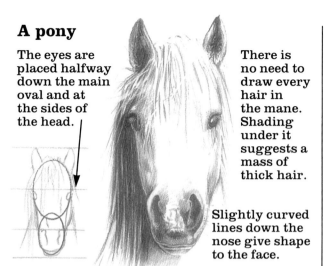

There is no need to draw every hair in the mane. Shading under it suggests a mass of thick hair.

Slightly curved lines down the nose give shape to the face.

Ponies have shorter, neater heads than horses. They often have dense coats and long, thick manes. Here, try using a fairly hard, 3H pencil for the outline and lighter shadows, with a softer HB for the darker ears, eyes, nostrils and mane.

A foal

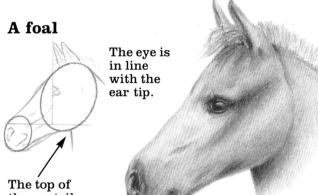

The eye is in line with the ear tip.

The top of the nostril is about level with the point where the head joins the neck.

Keep the outlines light for a soft look.

Foals have leaner, less well-defined heads than adults. The blue construction lines shown above will help you position the features correctly. As foals have fluffy coats and manes, a soft medium, such as colored pencil, works best.

A heavy horse

The creases in the neck are done in colored pencil.

Heavy horses * like this Suffolk Punch have thicker, broader heads and blunter muzzles than the lightweight breeds. Here, include the whole neck in the picture to increase the impression of the horse's massive size and muscle power.

A bridled head

Make the straps curve to show how they fasten around the whole head and to give a three-dimensional look to the face.

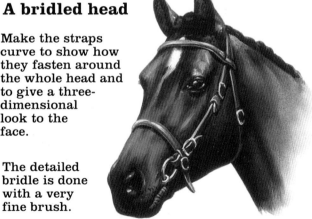

The detailed bridle is done with a very fine brush.

A bridle helps to frame and add character to the head. First draw the whole head and face in detail, then put in the bridle. Narrow straps look best on a refined head like this one, while a wide noseband and browband would suit a heavy horse better.

*Heavy horses, or coldbloods, are the biggest, strongest breeds and are mainly used for farm work or pulling heavy loads.

The gaits

Horses in motion make exciting pictures, but they can be tricky to draw. Here you can see a single moment from each of the four paces or gaits. Start with simple sketches like the one on the right to get the feel of the action.

Details can be added when the basic lines are right.

Walk

This is a smooth, gentle, four-beat gait in which the horse lifts and sets down each hoof in turn.

The neck is held long and relaxed.

Trot

In this springy, two-time motion, opposite legs, known as diagonals, are moved in unison. For example, the right foreleg and left hindleg are raised at the same time.

The head is carried high, but held still.

The neck is arched.

The tail floats slightly to give a sense of movement.

Canter

This is a bounding, rocking movement with three beats: the horse sets down one back hoof, then a pair of diagonals together, then the last front hoof.

The head is held high and swings as the horse moves.

The front legs come right up off the ground.

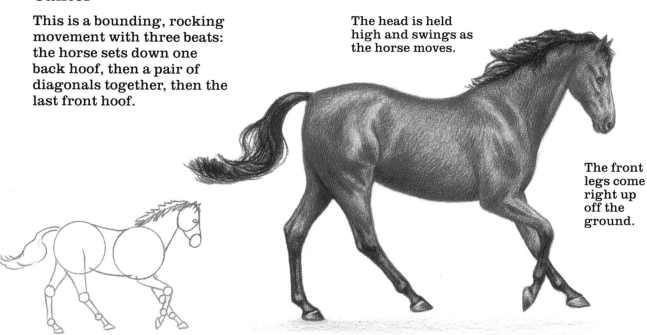

Gallop

This is the fastest and most dramatic gait, in which there is a moment, as here, when all four hooves are off the ground at the same time.

The streaming mane and tail show how fast the horse is going.

The neck and head are both extended out as the horse lunges forward.

Slightly blurred, directional pencil lines behind and above the horse increase the sense of movement.

A rearing horse

Horses are lively and can be nervous. They may rear if startled or excited. A horse rearing high on its hindlegs makes a dramatic picture. Here you can see how the watercolor horse on the opposite page was done, starting with the basic shapes shown on the right.

This foreleg is nearly at right angles with the weightline.

Draw a vertical weightline through the horse's hindquarters and hocks as shown. This will help make the horse appear properly balanced.

Try to keep the pencil lines smooth.

The mane and tail are the same color as the parts of the body from which they grow.

Smooth off the horse's outline and erase the circles and lines which will not appear on the final drawing. Draw the outline lightly. Mark in the edges of the piebald (black and white) patches, and sketch the eyes, nostrils and mouth.

Paint a base layer of violet or blue over where the black patches will be. This will give a rich sheen to the back. Give the hooves a layer of pale pink. Some dabs of pale gray in shadowy areas start to give shape to the white parts of the coat.

Build up the darker shades. Let the white paper and the violet base layer show through on the highlighted parts of the coat.

Pinky-beige watercolor and gray pencil stripes give the hooves shape.

Blend the edges of the black patches with a little gray paint to show where they merge with the white patches.

Only paint the parts of the horse which are in deep shadow solid black. You could touch up the highlights on the black areas with pale blue or violet pencils.

Where the muscles stand out, as on the legs and hindquarters, create contrast with dark lines and pale highlights. On the white patches, use some gray or yellowy-brown pencils to define the muscle lines.

As a finishing touch, streaks of white colored pencil prevent the tail from looking solid.

A bucking bronco

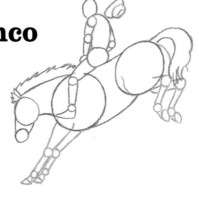

Bucking is a sign of high spirits, although broncos* like the one opposite use it to unseat their riders. Broncos are usually tame, but buck because they dislike being ridden. The picture was done in colored pencils. You can find out how it was done, and some hints on using colored pencils, on this page.

Start with the horse, then add the cowboy. His elbow, knee and boot tip form a straight line parallel with the line between the horse's shoulder and knee.

Do a simple line drawing, smoothing off the outline and erasing any lines you will not need in the final version. Add the outline of the shadow on the ground.

Put down a pale layer of golden yellow over the horse's coat. Try not to let the pencil strokes show, so that this layer looks as flat as possible. Put some gray and gold streaks into the mane and tail and apply some pale shading to the cowboy.

Add further layers of richer, darker shades. Consider which areas catch the light and which will be darker and add color accordingly. The sheen comes from letting the base layer shine through, so don't make these layers too solid.

Cowboys ride bucking broncos in competitions called rodeos. The cowboy tries to stay on for up to ten seconds, gripping with only one hand and his knees.

The picture is completed by adding the darkest colors to the parts of the horse and rider which are in shadow.

Use a sharp, dark pencil for fine features such as the eye.

The flying hat gives a sense of movement.

Let the paper show through where the pale tail catches the light.

A few movement lines around the bronco help to convey its jolting motion.

The shadow on the ground shows how high the horse's quarters are in the air.

Eventing

Eventing is one of the toughest of all horse sports. It involves horse and rider competing in three different disciplines: dressage*, cross country (speed and endurance) and show jumping. There is more about these on the next four pages, with some spectacular pictures to try.

Draw the shapes and lines of the horse first. The right foreleg and left hindleg are parallel.

The straight lines shown in green help you to find the height of the rider.

Dressage

A dressage test aims to show that the horse is highly obedient, supple and balanced and that the rider can control it easily. To do this, they have to perform various set movements.

The stillness of the rider contrasts nicely with the strong movement of the horse.

This horse and rider are performing an extended trot. The horse stays in a trotting rhythm, but stretches its legs more than usual.

The tail fluttering out adds a touch of freedom to the very controlled pose.

The horse's nose forms a vertical line parallel with the rider's position.

A long, dark shadow on the ground suggests how the horse is stretching out.

*This word comes from the French dresser, meaning to train.

Cross country (speed and endurance)

This is the most gruelling phase of an event. It involves riding at speed across country over lots of big jumps. Try copying this picture by laying some tracing paper over it and picking out the basic shapes and lines. Refine the outlines and transfer them to white paper before adding detail and color.

Use flecks of white paint for the flying water drops on the coat.

The rider's body is parallel with the horse.

Do the horse first. Use bold, strong lines to capture its powerful, surging movement.

A great splash of water gives a sense of the horse springing forward and up.

The water is a blend of light blue, green and purple. Let streaks of white show through to make it gleam.

15

Eventing: show jumping

The show jumping* stage of an event aims to test the horse's fitness and suppleness. Competitors have to clear a course of jumps which can involve lots of twists and turns between obstacles.

This picture uses gouache for a powerful, dynamic effect. It is drawn from low down, so that the viewer is looking up at the horse. This helps increase the sense of height and make the jump look impressive.

Sketch the horse first, then the rider. Put the jump in last. In the sketch on the right, the distance from the ears to the fetlocks is about the same as between the fetlocks and the base of the jump.

Working over the rough shapes, do an accurate pencil sketch of the horse, the rider and the jump. Erase the lines you don't need. Keep your pencil lines fairly light and try to keep the outline looking smooth and streamlined.

Paint a gray base coat, as shown on the hindquarters above, over the whole horse. Paint flat base coats over the jump and rider. Start to add paler highlights and darker shadows to the horse to give it form, as shown on the neck and shoulders.

*Show jumping is also a sport in its own right (see page 19).

Although the horse is black, only the darkest parts are painted solid black. Most of the coat is painted in shades of gray because lots of highlights make it look glossy. To find where highlights should go, imagine where the rounded parts would reflect the light.

The eye has a dot of white in it to make it look shiny.

Strong highlights, such as those on the glossy hindquarters, are almost white.

A highlight on the nearest knee makes it stand out from the one behind as well as making it look glossy.

Brushstrokes going in the direction of the growth of the coat help to make it look sleek and well-groomed.

Horse shows

These are gatherings in which horses and riders can take part in lots of different competitions or classes. Horse shows are usually big functions attracting people from far and wide, while gymkhanas tend to be smaller and include many mounted games which require speed and agility.

Showing

In a showing class, horses are judged according to their appearance, condition, movement and manners. See if you can copy this picture. The girl is riding sidesaddle, an old-fashioned style of seat in which both legs rest on the same side.

Both rider and pony are poised and have their heads raised so that they look confident and alert.

Use plenty of shadow on the skirt to suggest the draped layers of cloth.

Paint the pony first, using watercolor for a fairly soft effect. Let pale highlights show through to make its coat gleam. Then paint the rider with gouache for a more solid, detailed finish.

The rider carries a show cane.

The mane and forelock are done up in tiny, neat braids.

The double bridle, with two bits and two sets of reins, is traditional for showing.

This show pony has an excellent build, called its conformation. To help you get its proportions right, look at the tips on page 4.

Show jumping

This is one of the most popular of all equestrian sports. Specially built jumps are set up in an arena, and contestants must clear them in a particular order. This usually means the horse has to turn nimbly at various points in the course, so it needs to be very supple and agile as well as obedient.

Look closely at the construction lines shown below to see how the various parts of the pony and rider are positioned in relation to each other.

This picture is very dramatic because of the angle from which it is drawn. The strong contrast between the dark and light areas also adds to its impact. A quite hard, 3H pencil was used to shade the paler areas, while the eyes, jacket and boots were done in a softer HB.

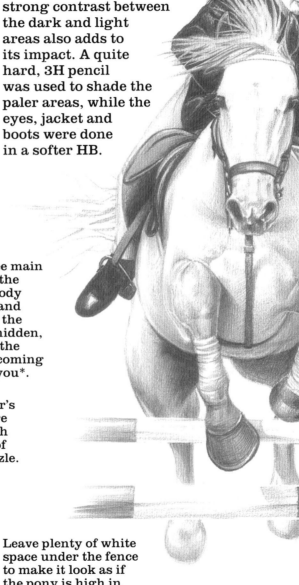

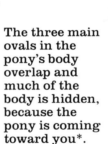

The three main ovals in the pony's body overlap and much of the body is hidden, because the pony is coming toward you*.

The rider's knees are level with the top of the muzzle.

Leave plenty of white space under the fence to make it look as if the pony is high in the air.

*This effect, where the body proportions are altered because of the angle from which the body is seen, is called foreshortening.

Cartoon horses

Horses work well as cartoons because of their big, expressive heads, gangly long legs and shaggy manes and tails. Here are some suggestions for ways to use these features to create comic effects, and opposite you can see how various horsy colours and markings can make a picture funny.

A carthorse

A smooth, bold outline gives the drawing more impact.

Apply a flat, gold base.

The "feather" on the horse's legs can be drawn like flared pantslegs.

Exaggerating the mouth into a grin adds humor.

With a soft pencil, such as a 2B, sketch the basic shapes as shown above left. Exaggerating the size of the head and features like the eyes and mouth adds a humorous touch.

When the outlines are right, go over them with a fine, black, waterproof felt tip pen. Finally, the coat color, shading and details should be added using colored inks or felt tips for a bright, solid effect.

A few extra hairs around the muzzle make it look shaggy.

Use long, wavy, black lines for the tail and feather.

Shadows can be added in ink or felt tip when the base is dry.

Highlights should be done last, in white ink or colored pencil.

Comical coat colors

Appaloosa

Skewbald

Different coat colors and markings creat different impressions, and here you can see three varieties which work particularly well in cartoons. Spotted Appaloosa horses look clownlike with their "rash" of irregular dark spots on a white face, and in fact are very popular in circuses. The broad brown-and-white patches of the skewbald make a funny, quirky pattern (see also the horse below), while a wide white blaze on a colored head adds a lot of character.

An old ranch horse

The back is slightly pointed where the old spine has weakened. A couple of hairs here make this stand out.

A missing tooth and some stray whiskers give a worn, dishevelled look.

Try copying this bony old horse by seeing if you can figure out the basic shapes for yourself (the body shapes on page 20 may help). To get the right sense of character, look closely at all the details, for example, the lumpy knees, the movement lines and the crossed eyes as the horse focuses on the carrot.

Large hooves on spindly legs give a plodding effect.

A few movement lines suggest the horse is unsteady on its feet.

21

Thelwell's cartoons

Norman Thelwell is a famous English cartoonist who has drawn many subjects, but is particularly well-known for his cartoons of horses and ponies. At first, he sold single cartoons to magazines and newspapers, but since 1957 he has produced lots of books, seven of which are just about ponies. His books are still hugely popular and are published all over the world.

Cross-hatching © 1965 Norman Thelwell.

Thelwell often draws in black ink with a fountain pen. This makes the details in the pictures show up clearly when printed.

Layers of short strokes are called cross-hatching. This technique is good for doing shadows. Here, they help to make the pony look plump.

Thelwell's style

© 1962 Norman Thelwell.

"HEEL!"

© 1957 Norman Thelwell.

Like all good cartoons, Thelwell's make an immediate impact. The picture above left works without words, because the idea is simple yet clever. This picture also uses strong contrasts, another feature of a lot of cartoon humor. For example, the difference between the smug, fat, smiling winner and the spiky, scowling loser is funny in itself. In a similar way, in the cartoon above right, the joke comes mainly from the fact that the pony is doing the opposite to what the rider is shouting.

Different pony characters

Exaggerating real-life details can also make cartoons funny. The labels around these pictures show how Thelwell uses humorous exaggeration in his cartoons, yet keeps the characters looking like real ponies. He always carries a sketchbook, so he can draw what he sees. You could do this to capture movements and expressions for your cartoons.

Shy, frightened pony

The big, staring eye and flaring nostril are based on real expressions, but exaggerated for comic effect.

The tiny size of the mouse which terrifies the pony is very funny.

© 1965 Norman Thelwell.

The rider tumbling off apparently unnoticed adds extra humor.

Snobby horse and rider

The horse's and rider's expressions mirror each other and intensify the haughty look.

The droopy reins bring out the long, thin neck.

© 1962 Norman Thelwell.

Bucking pony

This bucking pose is an exaggeration of the real thing (see page 13).

The naturally shaggy mane and tail are drawn as extravagant swirls.

The movement arcs give the impression of wild leaps and bounds.

© 1965 Norman Thelwell.

Drawing a moment in the trot when all four hooves are in the air makes the most of the springy action.

Making the rider and pony face in opposite directions shows how far they have come apart.

Details like the peaceful setting and the helpless onlookers contrast with the furious bucking.

23

Different breeds

It is fun and good practice to try drawing different breeds of horses or ponies, as each type has particular points that need to be brought out to get a realistic likeness. Here are pictures of four quite distinct breeds, showing their most notable features.

Arab

This is one of the most ancient, pure and beautiful of all breeds. It is a fairly small but compact, strong horse, full of grace and stamina. These qualities and its gentle nature make it very popular as both a show and riding horse.

Smooth, flowing lines suggest the Arab's springy and very graceful action.

The Arab's concave or "dished" face makes it easy to recognize. It has a broad forehead that tapers to a small muzzle.

The head and the flowing, silky tail are held high, giving a noble, lively effect.

Breton

This is a French heavy horse, used mainly for farm work. It has a sturdy, thickset build, with different proportions to the lightweight breeds. The legs, particularly, are much shorter than usual (try comparing them with the horse on pages 4-5). The head is squarish and set on a massive, short neck.

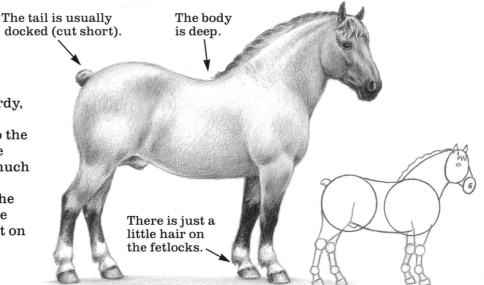

The tail is usually docked (cut short).

The body is deep.

There is just a little hair on the fetlocks.

24

Shetland pony

The Shetland is one of the smallest of the pony breeds, but is extremely strong and tough for its size. To capture the dense, fluffy look of its winter coat, do lots of short strokes very close together, or use colored pencils on a rough-surfaced paper.

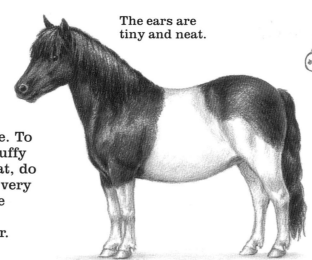

The ears are tiny and neat.

The body is compact and set on very short legs.

Long, wavy strokes give the mane and tail their full, shaggy look.

American Saddlebred

This spectacular horse is especially well known for its action. As well as the usual paces, it can be trained to do two extra gaits, including the rack. This is a flashy, exciting pace in which the horse moves each foot singly and in an even rhythm, but very fast. The Saddlebred carries its head and tail very high, giving it a spirited, elegant look which is unmistakable.

The head is refined and carried high on a long, curving neck.

The foal's head is much smaller than the adult's.

The tail sits high and gives a showy look.

The tail is short and fluffy.

The foal's legs are very long and slender in relation to its body.

The hooves are grown unusually long to draw attention to the horse's movement.

25

Horses at work

For thousands of years, people have used horses for all sorts of work because of their many different qualities. For example, the Percheron horses shown here are very powerful, yet docile and obedient.

Plowing

To copy this scene, first pencil in the horizon line. Then position the horses. Because they are coming toward you, it helps to sketch in the perspective lines shown in pink below. The farmer's height can be found by sketching a straight line level with and between the horses' backs, and extending this out to the horizon on the right-hand side of the picture.

A single tree here helps to balance the composition and adds interest to the bare field.

For the dapple horse, let the paper show through for the white face and spots. On the gray parts, use layers of watercolor, letting each one merge with the next for a mottled look.

The horses are foreshortened (see page 19), so the body circles of each one overlap.

The sky is a pale blue wash. For clouds, let the paper show through.

Adding some purple to the black of the horse's coat makes it look glossier.

To get a feeling of distance, make the grass paler as it gets closer to the tree-line.

Some birds swooping down for worms add a convincing touch.

Puffs of dust add a sense of movement.

The horses are the focus of the picture, so the plough need not be too detailed. It should be directly behind the team and lined up with the mid-point between the animals' chests.

Horses at rest

Horses are usually gentle, and this coupled with their graceful shapes can create lovely, tranquil pictures. As you draw these, try to make the lines flow. This gives a feeling of calm and makes the picture look alive even though the horses are still.

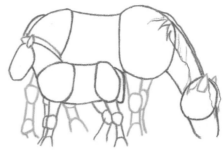

The foal looks gawky, with a big head in relation to its body, and long, gangly legs.

Grazing mare and foal

Pale blue and green washes make a peaceful background.

Strengthening the outline along the mare's back makes it stand out from the sky behind.

Soft shading on the mare's side, or flank, separates it from the foal.

For the shaggy white legs, let the paper show through. Touches of white paint make the hair look thicker, and tan streaks give shape to the legs.

The shadow links the horses and gives a sense of ground level. A blend of green and brown strokes works well.

Layers of yellow and brown watercolor give the horses' coats a warm glow.

These are heavy horses called Shires. Sketch the mare first, including all the parts that will eventually be hidden by the foal. This helps you understand exactly where each leg should be. Add the foal, then refine the outlines, keeping them soft and flowing. Color the picture in watercolor (as shown) or crayon. Pale yellow highlights on the mare's back, a shadow on the ground and a scatter of tiny flies above the mare's neck suggest the heat of a sunny summer afternoon.

Nuzzling

This makes a nice composition because the two Fjord ponies look like mirror-images of each other. Try copying the picture, using the method suggested on page 15. Draw all of the background pony first, then the foreground one, then the tree.

Next, paint the background with pale blue and green washes. For the ponies, use a fawn wash all over, then add the markings.

Soft dabs of lemon yellow and reddish brown for the leaves create a peaceful, gentle atmosphere.

Adding the dark brown of the legs while the base colour is damp blends it in softly.

Lying down

Horses can sleep standing up, and only lie down when they feel safe. Here, use light, soft lines to create a sense of peace. To paint the dappled coat, apply a pale gray wash. Let this dry. Dip a small piece of natural sponge in white paint and dab on the spots.

Yellow and orange streaks give the impression of a cozy, straw-strewn stable.

The heavy head hangs low as the horse dozes.

The ears are held back when the horse is dozing.

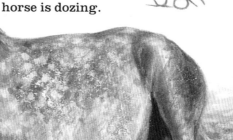

29

Mythical horses

As well as playing such an important part in people's lives as working animals, horses have also often appeared in legends and myths. Perhaps this is because their great beauty and power make them seem wonderful, almost magical creatures.

A very dark eye with a white highlight looks luminous and intelligent.

There is a small beard at the chin.

Curved, swirling lines for the mane and forelock give a romantic, magical feel.

The hooves are split, or cloven, like a goat's, and there is wavy, silky hair on the fetlocks.

The tail is like a lion's: long, smooth and muscular, with just a tassel of curly hair at the end.

Soft blue shading with watercolor paint makes the coat look clean and adds a shimmering, mysterious effect.

Unicorn

This lovely white horse with one horn in the middle of its forehead appears in the literature of Ancient Greece and in the art of the Middle Ages. It was said to be a rare, beautiful but wild animal, which could only be tamed by a young girl. To draw it, start as if it were an ordinary horse. The rearing pose shown on page 10 may help.